The
Guide to
Genetics

Gwen Acton

Oval Books

Published by Oval Books
5 St John's Buildings
Canterbury Crescent
London SW9 7QH
United Kingdom

Telephone: +44 (0)20 7733 8585
Fax: +44 (0)20 7733 8544
E-mail: info@ovalbooks.com
Web site: www.ovalbooks.com

Editors – Saffron Beatson & Pam Barrett
Series Editor – Anne Tauté

Cover designer – Vicki Towers
Cover image – Aris Multimedia Entertainment Inc., 1991-3
Printer – J F Print Ltd, Sparkford, Somerset.
Producer – Oval Projects Ltd.

The Bluffer's® Guides series is based
on an original idea by Peter Wolfe.

The Bluffer's Guide® , The Bluffer's Guides®,
Bluffer's®, and Bluff Your Way® are
Registered Trademarks.

ISBN: 978-1-903096-89-5

CONTENTS

INTRODUCTION

The best reason to become a bluffer in genetics is that you'll be popular at parties. The concept of heredity has been found irresistibly fascinating ever since it was first noticed that kids tend to look more like their parents than, say, goats. (Unless their parents were goats.)

> **The concept of heredity has been found irresistibly fascinating ever since it was first noticed that kids tend to look more like their parents than, say, goats.**

The fast-paced advances in the field of genetics will make your bluffing all the easier because no-one can really keep up with it all. It also kindles a slew of legal and ethical issues – such as those relating to stem cells, cloning, and genetically modified food – that can lead to hours of successful bluffing with very little exertion on your part, since there is always another side to the matter that can be raised, and few right answers (other than your own, that is).

The more bluffing you do, the more people will gather around you, both to be impressed, but also to argue. In fact, you will find that most people believe they are already an expert in genetics because (1) they were born with genes, or (2) they suspect that they have better genes than everyone else and want to find out for sure.

This book will provide you with all the necessary tools to successfully handle such non-professionals. Contrary to what you might fear, it is easily accomplished. Geneticists, like most scientists, love to use complicated terminology in what might otherwise be perfectly straightforward explanations. So, throw out a few choice terms, such as **SNP**s (pronounced 'snips') and therapeutic cloning, follow some simple bluffing strategies, such as avoiding certain topics altogether, and you will be well on your way to improving your social prospects. It may also have the added benefit of making you more attractive to potential mates who will be interested in having your brilliance passed on to their offspring. That is, if you can successfully convince them that your prowess is truly genetic.

> **66** Throw out a few choice terms such as SNPs (pronounced 'snips') and you will be well on your way to improving your social prospects. **99**

EARLY HISTORY

A convenient way to get a handle on genetics is through its history. The subject has the added advantage that you can confidently discuss it by making up just about any absurd theory you want –

such as that animals can be fertilised by the wind (the Romans came up with that one) or that maggots arise spontaneously from rotting meat (popular in Europe during the middle ages). And someone, somewhere, probably believed it.

One remarkable thing about the study of **heredity** is how amazingly long it took to figure out. However, like many human endeavours, lack of understanding didn't prevent people from practising it anyway. Archaeological evidence suggests that as humans first began settling in villages thousands of years ago, they picked out seeds from plants that were tastier, juicier or otherwise more desirable, and planted more of them the next year, improving the species to their liking.

This type of selective breeding, which you should make sure to call 'artificial selection', was also practised for millennia on animals. By breeding more of the milkiest cow, the tastiest pig, or the woolliest sheep, over time domesticated animals came to look less and less like their wild counterparts, and more like the docile, meaty and practical animals that adorn farms today. You can point out that people apparently also modified animals in this way for the sheer hell of it, as evidenced by the Chihuahua.

> **" The history of genetics has the added advantage that you can discuss it by making up just about any theory you want. "**

Greek guesses

Toss out the names of a few Greek philosophers to lend yourself an air of plausibility. Hippocrates is a good one. Around 400 B.C. he recognised that the male contribution to heredity is found in semen. He then logically assumed that there must be a similar fluid in women, and that these fluids were made throughout the body and collected in the reproductive organs. So, for example, he reasoned that the semen from the head had the materials to make a new head. At conception, the fluids would come together, from the man and woman, and would battle with each other (like minuscule fistfights) to see which one won.

> **66 Aristotle believed that men with long penises were less fertile. 99**

Surprisingly, ensuing theories of heredity managed to go downhill from there. Aristotle believed that male semen alone determined the form of the offspring, while females were created by interference from the mother's blood. (You might wonder aloud that his motives on this particular topic weren't questioned more closely, since he also thought that men with long penises were less fertile.)

Births and blends

From Roman times until the late 19th century, it was generally accepted that life could arise spontaneously from non-living, often decaying, matter. A

17th-century recipe for 'spontaneous generation' required placing dirty underwear and wheat husks in an open-mouthed jar, and then waiting three weeks until the sweat from the undergarments transformed the plant material into mice.

Fast forward to the 1700s when Dutch scientist Anton van Leeuwenhoek (Lay-van-hook) was able to use an early microscope to study sperm. What he saw convinced him that each sperm contained a 'homunculus', a very tiny version of a human curled up inside (which is not far off when you come to think of it). This led to a movement called the spermists who believed that the sole contribution of females to the next generation was the womb in which the homunculus would grow.

> **What he saw convinced him that each sperm contained a very tiny version of a human curled up inside (which is not far off when you come to think of it).**

To avoid unpleasantness, be quick to explain that there was an opposing school of thought led by the ovists who believed the future human was in the egg, and that the role of sperm was merely to stimulate the growth of the egg. Ovists were certain that the eggs contained little boys or girls, so the gender was settled even before conception. Both ovists and spermists are considered preformationists since they assumed that the person is 'pre-formed' before fertilisation, rather than acquiring convenient attributes like legs, arms, and toes after egg meets sperm.

Since the spermist and ovist theories were very hard to support in the light of heaps of evidence that children often look like a combination of both their parents, other groups in the 19th century came up with blending theories of inheritance. They reasoned that mixing sperm and eggs resulted in offspring that were a 'blend' of the two parents' characteristics. For example, if a red flower were mated with a white flower, the resulting blooms would be pink. While this is often the case, the theory utterly failed to explain why sometimes the offspring look like one or the other, or neither of the parents but are the spitting image of grandma, and why people aren't all a blended bunch of look-alikes. Theorists, it should be kept in mind, are seldom deterred by the facts.

> **66 They reasoned that mixing sperm and eggs resulted in offspring that were a 'blend'. 99**

The marvel that was Mendel

The true beginning of the field of genetics is credited to an Austrian monk named Gregor Mendel who made a practice of breeding peas in his monastery garden, and then carefully counting the types of offspring that resulted. He published his results in

1866, but, possibly because his approach was quite mathematical, which wasn't any more popular then than it is now, they were ignored during his lifetime (which has to be incredibly frustrating, even for a monk).

Mendel's biggest discovery (and the reason he is credited with founding the field of genetics) is that heredity is determined by distinct units, which were later named genes. This

66 Mendel mated (but always say crossed) male green peas with female yellow peas, and female green peas with male yellow peas. 99

was in contrast to previous theories, such as the blending hypothesis, because it meant the units could be passed down through the generations without change, even if they didn't appear in a particular generation.

Mendel was also able to settle the debate between the ovists and spermists by switching around the sexes of the parental generation. It turns out (surprise, surprise) that they were both wrong. For example, Mendel mated (but always say **crossed**) male green peas with female yellow peas, and female green peas with male yellow peas. He discovered that these so-called **reciprocal crosses** didn't make a darned bit of difference to the outcome.

The bluffer should be comfortable with the fact that Mendel came up with 'laws'. If you don't understand them, don't worry. They aren't even always true. Just call them 'Mendel's First Law' and 'Mendel's Second Law'. You can pass off any vexing questions about them with a wave of your hand and say that they are better understood through molecular genetics, which happens to be both convenient, and true.

NATURE VERSUS NURTURE

Though the field of genetics is all about the study of heredity, an excellent way to establish your credibility is to raise the issue of whether human beings are primarily controlled by nature (i.e., genetics) or by nurture (i.e., environment). Rest assured that you will be perfectly safe in taking either side or neither. Many wise people have pondered the point without reaching any satisfactory conclusions. So nor need you.

> **66 Rest assured that you will be perfectly safe in taking either side or neither. 99**

This subject has the added advantage that you do not have to know any actual facts in order to have an opinion. And if you want to side-step the issue, take the neutral route by stating that human beings are clearly a product of both. Providing an example can prove helpful at this point. It is known that people's height is a product of both what they eat, and the genes they inherited (so consuming more vegetables might make someone taller, but probably not enough for professional basketball). At the other end of the spectrum, the shapes and sizes of noses are determined by genetics (although the tendency of proboscises of all descriptions to be stuck into other people's business is another matter).

> **66 Consuming more vegetables might make someone taller, but probably not enough for professional basketball. 99**

Even on these points you can successfully quibble if someone other than you brings them up. (This is the splendid thing about this topic.) Since both nature and nurture have a bearing on how things turn out, bring up the concept of **heritability**. The heritability of very little is known with certainty, so you can speculate at will as long as the number is somewhere between 0% (non-genetic) and 100% (genetic), as in "The heritability of your paranoid personality is estimated to be 50%, which proves they could indeed be out to get you", or toss out some of the published (but not necessarily proven) numbers:

- height (85%)
- weight (70%)
- personality (50%)
- scholastic achievement (38%)
- memory (20%) – (except the ability to recall anniversaries and the whereabouts of the car keys).

While on the nature/nurture subject, don't miss the opportunity to infuse the conversation with the words:

- **genotype** (jean-oh-type) – the seasoned geneticist's term for genetic make-up;
- **phenotype** (fee-no-type) – a term used when referring to the appearance of a living entity, as in: "The phenotype of that man is short, fat and balding."

To successfully carry off the bluff, you must remember that two beings can have the same genotype, but (due to environmental influences) different phenotypes. For example, the short, fat, balding man may have an identical twin (same genotype) who is tall and thin due to eating more spinach as a child. The tall twin probably also displays some scalp since most patterned hair loss is highly heritable. Although even here you never know – he may have altered his phenotype using hair transplants.

GENES

DNA basics

Since the goal of the bluffer is to expend as little effort as possible in understanding the underlying science of genetics, but to sound as if he or she does this for a living, or lives with someone who does, we must now put you in the enviable position of being a plausible professional on the basic substance of genes and heredity. The key point to grasp is that they are composed of **DNA** (for which you might find occasion to use the full term deoxyribonucleic acid [dee-ox-ee-rye-bow-new-clay-ik acid) or, as those who cracked the code proclaimed: The Secret of Life.

To make yourself sound even more proficient, liberally toss around the term **genome** ('jean-gnome') to describe all the genes and DNA in a species. To cover up your lack of laboratory time, we have also added some 'DNA distractions', each one sufficient to amaze the toughest audience.

To be up and running as a DNA expert, it is best to think of it as resembling a zip (or zipper if you're American). You

> **❝ As a plausible professional on DNA you might find occasion to use the full term – deoxyribonucleic acid. ❞**

just need to call each side of the zip a **strand** and call its teeth **bases**. There are only four types of bases that need concern you. These you will nonchalantly refer to as A, T, C, and G. (Fortunately, it is not necessary to cite the bases by their full names – Adenine, Thymine, Cytosine and Guanine – as only amateurs bother with that.)

When you have taken your audience this far, you will certainly need some of our patent distractions:

DNA distraction (i) Each base is about one millionth of a centimetre wide, rendering it invisible except through powerful microscopes. Nevertheless, some companies offer to incorporate into jewellery the DNA of loved ones, pets, and celebrities, proving it really is the thought that counts.

If you think a zip with four types of teeth sounds entirely too simple to be the fundamental spark of life then you are in good company. Scientists world-wide ignored the early evidence for DNA being the basis of heredity for about a decade because they could not fathom how a long strand of so few types of bases could be responsible for carrying the information for such complex structures as a hip joint, a nostril, or a brain that can think about baseball.

> **Some companies offer to incorporate into jewellery the DNA of loved ones, pets, and celebrities, proving it really is the thought that counts.**

A breakthrough came when it was realised that it was the order of the four types of bases where all the action was occurring. It is this order or **sequence** that provides the crucial genetic information to the 'organism'. (The latter term, which is popular among scientists, should be used wherever you can as it refers to forms of life of every shape, size and kind, and is enhanced by sounding similar to other pleasurable diversions.)

DNA unravelled

While most zips are fairly straight, each strand of the DNA is in the form of a helix, which is the shape made by the twirl that goes round and round the common or garden screw. The two DNA strands are bonded together by their bases and are twisted around each other to produce the famous **double helix** shape and, like humans, they like to bond in pairs: A with T and C with G. A handy aid to remember this is that As and Ts are angular, pointy letters, while Cs and Gs are fat, round letters. Or keep in mind the phrase 'Ants Teeth Cannot Grind'.

Assert that the sequence of one strand will always correspond – or in technical terms, be complementary – to the other since an A or C on one strand means a T or G must occur on the other, and vice versa. For example, if one strand is GTA, then the other strand must be CAT.

This talk of strands can lead you neatly to:

DNA distraction (ii) Now state that human beings have 3,000 million base pairs– or 3,000 megabases if you think that sounds more impressive – the salamander has 24,000 million, and the lily has 91,000 million (which gives new meaning to the biblical exhortation to "consider the lilies…").

Be sure to observe that the complementarity of DNA is the fundamental aspect that allows it to pass on genetic information from generation to generation: unzip (unwind) a double helix, and each strand has the information to copy or replicate the second strand. This means you have two identical double helixes (zips) where you only had one before.

DNA distraction (iii) DNA has 'semi-conservative' replication; this has nothing to do with politics, although you can always try to claim it does. It simply means the two newly formed double helixes each have one old and one new strand of DNA.

DNA replicating

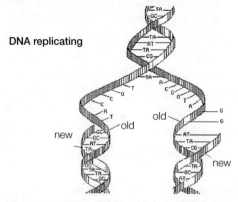

new old old new

DNA distraction (iv) When DNA gets too tightly wound up, or twisted, then enzymes, called topo-isomerases (toe-poe-eye-som-er-aces) get to work, like a good masseuse, to relax the DNA. Go ahead and make an analogy to unwinding after a hard day.

Packing DNA

Having mastered the double helix, you now rise to the next level and consider where all this fits in, and fitting is the key. DNA is packed away in **chromosomes**, each one containing one long DNA (ranging from 50 million bases to 250 million bases long in humans) wrapped around some proteins (or nucleosomes to those in the know) to keep it from getting tangled up.

> **The result is a packing strategy known as supercoiling, rather like the one used to get the last pair of shorts into the corner.**

You are advised not to dwell on the figures but instead to remark on the pleasing similarity with the problem of your suitcase the night before you are due to go on holiday. The result, in the case of DNA, is a packing strategy known as **supercoiling**, rather like the one used to get the last pair of shorts into the corner.

Good things often come in pairs. And so it is with DNA. In other words, one good chromosome deserves another. Humans have 23 pairs, or 46 chromosomes in each **cell** in the body. One of each pair came from the mother, one from the father.

The chromosomes are numbered from largest to smallest, so that the longest chromosome is 1, slightly smaller is 2, etc. Except, that is, for one naming mistake: chromosome 21 is actually smaller than chromosome 22 simply because it took several decades to realise that there was another pair. (Be grateful the body is better at keeping track.)

Geneticists call chromosomes 1 to 22 the autosomes. The remaining pair are sex chromosomes, not chromosomes for having sex but chromosomes that determine the sex of individuals – either two Xs for a girl, or an X and a Y for a boy. This process can also be referred to for bluffing effect as 'sex determination'.

> **The remaining pair are sex chromosomes, not chromosomes for having sex but chromosomes that determine the sex of individuals.**

Chromosomes, in turn, are packed into cells (from the Latin *'cellua'* which means small compartment), which you airily refer to as the "microscopic basic building blocks" of all life forms. A great distraction at this point is to mention the number of chromosomes in other species:

Bacteria: 1 chromosome
Mosquito: 6 chromosomes
Cat: 38 chromosomes
Dog: 78 chromosomes
King crab: 208 chromosomes

You might comment wryly that this would seem to indicate that chromosome number and intelligence are not related (although one might never know for certain in the case of the crab).

How genes work, or don't

Another reason it took so long to realise DNA held such great importance is that though DNA can't do much by itself it holds information in the form of **genes** enough to create life of every sort on earth. It's important at this stage to recognize that one can use the term 'gene' to mean either:

a a unit of heredity that carries information from one generation to the next;

b a bit of DNA that carries information for that particular organism.

Geneticists use the two concepts of the gene simultaneously and interchangeably, even when they contradict each other in certain contexts. This does not bother geneticists, so under no circumstances should you reveal any discomfort yourself.

> **If bases were indeed the size of zip teeth, this would be about 6,000 kilometres (3,600 miles) in length.**

Each gene is nothing more than a length of DNA in a chromosome of around 3,000 base pairs (teeth) long*. (If bases were indeed the size of zip teeth, this would be about 6,000 kilometres (3,600 miles) in length, which gives

---

* If called to account about this, respond (with a slight curl of the lip) that this is an approximate average and that you are fully aware, of course, that genes can be interrupted.

you an idea of how much longer DNA is than it is wide.). In the human genome there are thought to be around 20,000 genes – a number that is so uncertain in the scientific community as to be the subject of after-hours betting pools.

> **Approximately 98% of DNA is referred to as 'junk' because it has no known function.**

It does not take a mathematical mind to calculate that 20,000 genes times 3,000 base pairs is only 60 million, or about 2% of the 3 thousand million base pairs in the human genome. The other approximately 98% of DNA is referred to as **junk** because it has no known function. Feel free to speculate wildly about whether it really has no purpose, or whether its value is yet to be discovered.

The bases of a gene are organised in sets of three (e.g. GGG, CCC or TTA, etc.), known in expert echelons as codons or triplets. The body 'translates' (the official term) the DNA into something useful by using each three-base codon to make one of 20 amino acids. Which three bases corresponds to which amino acid is the **genetic code**. It was this code that was deciphered (or you can say 'broken') in 1961 by U.S. scientist Marshall Nirenberg who successfully beat a competing club of 20 hotshot researchers so devoted to the problem that each wore a diagram of a different amino acid on his tie.

The genetic code is considered 'universal' because it is essentially the same in all known life, meaning that a codon for a certain amino acid in humans is identical to that in aardvarks, mushrooms, sponges or dandelions.

DNA distraction (v) The genetic code is also said to be degenerate. With 64 possible codons and only 20 amino acids, more than one codon codes for each amino acid. Alternatively, you can call them redundant, although to call something so universal both degenerate and redundant might be thought a bit extreme.

DNA distraction (vi) Three of the codons serve as signals to end a gene, and these 'stop' codons have names. The first to be discovered, TAG, was named 'amber' after its discoverer, Harris Bernstein, whose surname means amber in German. The other two stop codons were then named 'ochre' and 'opal', colourfully illustrating scientific humour.

> **❝ The bases of a gene are organised in sets of three known in expert echelons as codons or triplets. ❞**

The amino acids in turn are used by the body to make proteins. You have arrived – everybody will recognise the word 'protein'.

Next to take on board is that one gene provides

the information to make one protein. If anyone nit picks about this not always being true, avoid an argument by simply saying you have not forgotten about 'alternative splicing' but think it is overrated, and leave it at that.

To move the conversation along, it is sometimes useful to drop some colourful protein names such as:

Botulinum toxin: Also known as Botox, it is one of the most poisonous naturally occurring substances in the world. Found in certain bacteria, and today used cosmetically to disguise wrinkles.

Rubisco: Thought to be the most abundant protein on earth, it is required by plants to turn sunlight and air into energy to grow. It is somewhat inefficient, which is why leaves have so much of it.

Luciferase: The substance that allows fireflies to light up at night, now also used in research to make other animals glow.

Conantokin: a protein found in the venom of the fish-hunting Conus snails. When given to mice, it has the interesting effect of causing young ones to fall asleep but older ones to become hyperactive.

Sonic Hedgehog: a key player in the human body's ability to make fingers and brains. Scientists and clinicians have since tried to change the name thinking it too frivolous because it refers to a computer game character, but it remains.

Doublesex: There really is a gene position, or **locus**, that produces a protein by this name, and it is surely asking too much of any bluffer not to improvise on that theme. (The fact that this is only a fruit fly protein concerned with male–female differentiation need not deter you: your audience will never know.)

Now you come to the last refinements. In order for the protein-making process to work, some of the genes must be turned 'on' and others turned 'off', a process known suggestively as 'gene expression'. Try to resist the temptation to make jokes about genes discussing their feelings, especially when you add that there are enhancers that turn them on, and suppressors that shut them off.

> **❝Some of the genes must be turned 'on' and others turned 'off', a process known suggestively as 'gene expression'.❞**

DNA distraction (vii) Not all the genes are expressed or turned 'on' (i.e. making proteins) all the time. If they were, then there would be no differences between, say, a hand and an eyeball (which might make seeing quite challenging, and bouncing a ball quite painful).

LATER HISTORY

Heredity heretics

Things took a real leap forward in 1900 when Mendel's work was rediscovered independently by three different European scientists (who must have been rather vexed to be tied three-ways for second place without even the possibility of the winner being disqualified for drug doping). Two years later Walter Sutton came up with the proposal that chromosomes are the **carriers** of heredity.

> **The first decade of the century was a great one for fruit flies, at least from a scientific perspective.**

The term 'genetics', from the Greek *genos*, meaning birth, was invented by the British scientist William Bateson in 1905. Ironically, the word 'gene' itself was not coined until four years later by Danish botanist Wilhelm Johannsen.

The first decade of the century was a great one for fruit flies, at least from a scientific perspective. Thomas Hunt Morgan used them to show that genes are indeed carried on chromosomes. Other scientists, such as Alfred Sturtevant, Hermann Muller and Calvin Bridges soon noticed that genes are usually physically linked to each other in such a way that they are often inherited together. Except when they aren't, which they attributed to '**recombination**', or the process by which chromosomes exchange bits of themselves with each other. You can claim that these processes hold true in humans as well, since it has long been observed that blue eyes and light-coloured hair are often associated with each other, but not always.

It was also quickly discovered that genes are located in essentially the same place (but call it 'the locus') on particular chromosomes in all individuals

66 If two specific genes are next to each other in, say, Madonna, then they will be in the same locus in the Pope. 99

of a species. This means that genes can be 'mapped' relative to one another, by describing their location and order on chromosomes. So if two specific genes are next to each other on a region of chromosome 17 in, say, Madonna (Queen of Pop), then they will be in the same locus in the Pope as well.

Genetics revealed a dark side at this time when there were many proponents of Eugenics, the notion that people can be made 'better' through controlled breeding. Not only did this turn out to be scientifically unfeasible, but everyone knows that humans are perfect as they are (or at least as you are).

The basis of bases

The lingering question was exactly which component of the chromosome – proteins or DNA, since they are made of both – was the physical basis of heredity.

Surprisingly, as early as 1943 compelling evidence from careful experiments conducted by American Oswald Avery implicated DNA, since it could transfer genetic traits to bacteria. But his work was dismissed and largely ignored because the prejudice was so strongly in favour of proteins. After all, proteins can exist in a myriad forms and functions, from hair and muscle, to egg whites and enzymes, while DNA, made of only four building blocks, just sits calmly in the nucleus.

> **❝ Crick and Watson were pitted against an international array of more experienced and famous scientists, including Nobel Prize-winner Linus Pauling. ❞**

Entertain your audience with the genetics cliff-hanger contest that emerged from the effort to discover the structure of DNA. The dark horses were brash American James Watson and British war veteran Francis Crick, who were considered too young and inexperienced to be taken seriously. They were pitted against an international array of more experienced and famous scientists, including Nobel Prize-winner Linus Pauling, a renowned structural chemist, and odds-on favourite to beat the rest of the pack.

Crick and Watson succeeded in part by 'borrowing' (without her permission) X-ray data from fellow scientist Rosalind Franklin, who was working at King's College with Maurice Wilkins (who ended up collecting the Nobel Prize along with Crick and Watson). Pauling lost the challenge in part due to the embarrassing mistake of constructing a model of DNA that violated basic chemistry laws taught in introductory classes – an error for which he would certainly have failed his own students.

The molecular era

The next few decades focused on better understanding how genes actually function. It was discovered that proteins are not actually made *directly* from genes in the DNA (that would be entirely too simple and straightforward). Instead there is an intermediary substance similar in structure to DNA, called **RNA** (Ribonucleic Acid). It was this finding that enabled geneticists to develop the impressive sounding Central Dogma, which outlines how information flows in the process of making a gene, as follows:

> **"Point out, knowingly, that despite its name the Central Dogma is not always true. "**

$$DNA \rightarrow RNA \rightarrow Protein$$

In fact, it's a bluff. Point out, knowingly, that despite its name the Central Dogma is not always true. If pressed, give the example that RNA can function as the gene product itself with no protein being made. Beyond this, the topic of RNA gets rather tricky so if it arises you are advised simply to mention the recent discoveries in 'interfering' RNA (or RNAi if you prefer). RNAi, you can proclaim, is used by scientists to reduce or 'knock down' (the technical term) gene expression both for research experiments (to see what the gene does) and possible therapeutic purposes. Be careful not to confuse it with the entirely different 'antisense' RNA – which would not make sense anyway.

The human genome project

In the 1970s methods were developed to determine the sequence of the As, Ts, Cs, and Gs in DNA. This exciting advance at last allowed scientists to 'read' genes, and two decades later technology had progressed to the point where it was possible to contemplate deciphering the complete human 'Book of Life'. To give some sense of the enormity of the project, make the point that it would take

❝ It would take about 100 years to read out loud (without stopping) all the bases in a person's genome sequence if you read one base per second. ❞

about 100 years to read out loud (without stopping) all the bases in a person's genome sequence if you read one base per second.

With very little preparation, you can embellish this momentous undertaking with the same level of excitement as an international sports tournament. It is competitive science at its best, complete with controversy, passion, and ultimately a winner (or more accurately, many winners). The not-for-profit Human Genome Project was a multi-national group of hundreds of scientists organised (to the degree any group of scientists can be organised, which is quite nominal) by the U.S. National Institutes of Health.

66 The competitive nature of the project had the incidental benefit that the government-led effort came in years ahead of schedule. 99

After initial concerns over the dangers of Big Science and various squabbles, it hummed along as an internationally government-funded enterprise for its first eight years. Then the situation heated up spectacularly when the for-profit company Celera announced its aim to complete the job earlier than the government's efforts, potentially scooping this opportunity for glory, and raising concerns about costly or restricted access to genome information.

Several years of heroic endeavour ensued. In the end (the competitive nature of the project having had the incidental benefit that the government-led effort came in years ahead of its original schedule), the race was proclaimed a tie, complete with joint press conferences and mutual congratulations.

In 2003 – fortuitously the 50th anniversary of the discovery of the DNA helix – the human genome

27

sequence was declared 'completed'. In truth, this was a somewhat arbitrary designation, as there remain regions of the genome that are not yet known (though you will want to say "have not been fully sequenced") and the exact number and location of genes have yet to be "fully determined". Nonetheless, since the vast majority of the genome had been deciphered at that point scientists claimed 'victory'. The result was a complete catalogue of all (well, nearly all) human genes, a veritable 'blueprint for life'.

> **The Human Microbiome Project seeks to sequence all the bacteria and other microscopic organisms that live on and in people (including those in guts, navels, and the crooks of elbows).**

Among other milestones there are a couple that will intrigue those around you. One is determining the sequence of a menagerie of species such as the fruit fly, chimp, dog, rat, mouse, chicken, platypus, round worm, and a wide variety of fungi. The other is the Human Microbiome (micro-buy-ome) Project, which seeks to sequence the entire entourage of all the (usually) harmless bacteria and other microscopic organisms that live on and in people (including those in guts, navels, and the crooks of elbows). Don't miss the opportunity to emphasize that these microbes collectively possess at least 100 times as many genes as their human hosts.

Playing with genes

Science progressed rapidly in the final decades of the 20th century to the point where genes could be changed, moved and manipulated, in other words engineered. Researchers in California developed methods to splice together or 'recombine' DNA from different organisms (so call it 'recombinant DNA technology'). In 1973 DNA was transferred for the first time from one life form to another. It was only microscopic bacteria, but it opened the doors to a new direction.

66 In 1994, the first genetically modified (GM) food product, the Flavr Savr tomato, gained approval for sale. 99

In 1994, the first genetically modified (GM) food product, the Flavr Savr tomato, gained approval for sale in the United States. Its modification was that one of the ripening genes was turned off, resulting in firmer, more flavourful tomatoes that could be left on the vine longer before shipping and still show up intact on the grocery shelves.

Ongoing research in the growing field of 'biotechnology' includes gene 'chips' – not the fattening kind but robotically manufactured devices that enable researchers simultaneously to measure the expression of all genes in the body. Gene chips play a vital role in 'personalised medicine', the highly-anticipated effort to predict how people will respond to drugs based on their genes.

To aid you in enthusing about the expanding boundaries of chemistry and life here are a few highlights:

- Scientists have succeeded in synthesising from scratch the first bacterial genome in the laboratory, heralding the new era of 'synthetic' biology. Interesting applications include building bacteria that smell like bananas and mint.
- Designing plant genes that can be switched on by sound waves, so that some day desirable genetic traits might be switched on in crops by blasting sound into farm fields.
- Genetically tinkering with nerve cells to make them respond to laser light, so that fruit flies can be made to leap, mice to twirl, and worms to stop squirming just by turning on a light switch.

Forms of genes

Efforts are now focused on being able to sequence genomes more quickly and cheaply. It is already possible for individuals to have their entire genomes read for an outrageous price, or parts of their genomes sequenced at a more reasonable fee. The value of such information, at whatever cost, is a matter of debate since the so-called 'post-genome' world of genetics involves trying to figure out how differences in DNA correlate with changes in heredity – a problem that has proved more difficult than was originally hoped.

Inform your listeners that they can now appreciate that a single change in a base pair of DNA can have enormous consequences depending on where it is located. If, for example, it occurs inside a gene, it may change the resulting protein. Toss out an example to prove your point: a Japanese research team has found that the switch of a single DNA base pair (from G–C to A–T) in the earwax gene on chromosome 16 determines whether a person has wet or dry earwax.

It is imperative in genetics bluffing that you use the word **allele** ("ah-leel") – plural, alleles – a good deal to describe these different possible forms or variations of a gene. For example, the earwax gene (also known to geneticists by the tongue-twisting name 'ATP-binding cassette C11' or ABCC11 for ease of reference) can produce earwax in a wet allele (i.e. form) or a dry allele. One gene, two different alleles – wet and dry. This is a fun fact to use as it has the advantage that you can make others look ridiculous by encouraging them to stick their fingers in their ears to figure out which they have.

> **The switch of a single DNA basepair (from G–C to A–T) in the earwax gene on chromosome 16 determines whether a person has wet or dry earwax.**

Two are better than one

Human chromosomes come in pairs, and genes are a component of chromosomes, therefore people have two of each gene – one on the chromosome from mum, one from dear old dad (or possibly someone else's). Note that though they are actually 'in' the chromosomes, geneticists always say 'on', and so, therefore, should you. The two so-called 'copies' of a gene in a person can both be the same variety (but say allele) of the gene, or two different varieties.

If the two inherited copies of the gene are the same, for example, wet earwax alleles from both mum and dad (wet/wet), trot out the term **homozygote** (homo-zie-goat – *homo* from the Greek meaning same) to describe them. And if a person inherits different copies of the alleles (wet/dry) you will, naturally, call them **heterozygotes** (hetero-zie-goats – from the Greek word *hetero* meaning different).

> **66** Someone can be a homozygote for one gene and a heterozygote for another gene at the same time and still be able to walk and chew gum too. **99**

But someone can, at the same time, be a homozygote for one gene (e.g. second toe length), and a heterozygote for another gene (e.g. earwax) and still be able to walk and chew gum too.

Determinedly dominant

Not all alleles of a gene are created equal. Some, it turns out, are more equal than others. In the political life of inheritance, some alleles are said to be dominant over others, and the ones they bully are recessive. This only happens in a heterozygote of course because of the difference in alleles, and the only way anyone can work out which is which is to let them fight it out.

> **The dominant allele is the one that determines what the person looks like.**

The dominant allele is the one that determines what the person looks like: indeed, the recessive does not even show up in the phenotype of the individual if the dominant is there. It is quite a good idea to give an example here, and throw in as many genetics terms as possible so it sounds more complicated.

For instance, wet earwax is dominant to dry. Therefore if someone is a heterozygote for the earwax gene, he or she will have wet earwax: though the person has one of each type of allele, the wet allele (G) is dominant and wins out over the dry allele (A) – better serving its role in preventing dust and insects from entering the ear, although it also apparently causes more armpit sweat and consequently more body odour as well.

This multiplicity of effects provides the bluffer with an excellent opportunity to use the splendid

33

term 'pleiotropic' (plee-oh-trope-ick) in connection with the earwax gene since it is a single gene that influences many characteristics.

Here are some other examples of intriguing traits determined by a single gene, should you need to use them to avoid awkward questions:

- 'Tongue rolling' is dominant over the lamentable inability to curl it, a skill critical for the social life of 6-year-olds.

- Unattached earlobes are dominant to attached earlobes, which does not seem to affect how many piercings the ears can support.

- Having freckles (adorable, except when they aren't) is dominant to not having them.

- A straight thumb is dominant to the so-called 'hyperextensible' or hitchhiker's thumb, which allows this digit to bend backwards (at least 45 degrees), presumably increasing the odds of getting picked up when displaying it.

- A big toe (hallux) shorter than the second toe is recessive to having a hallux longer than the toe next to it, except if you happen to be a Greek god (which is why a longer second digit is sometimes called a Greek foot). So, if your second toe is longer than your big toe, you inherited the Greek foot/Greek foot i.e., recessive/recessive alleles of the gene.

- Left over right interlocking fingers is dominant to right over left. Get people to clasp their hands together without thinking and check if the left or right thumb is on top, but don't get too exercised about this as it is of dubious scientific validity.

You will soon realise, even without any obfuscation on your part, that people mistakenly believe that if something is dominant it means that it is more common. The best way to win this strategic point is by giving them a counter-example they can see at face value – for instance, that chin fissures such as are found in actors Michael and Kirk Douglas are dominant, but rare (except perhaps in film stars). So being a bully makes an allele (variant) neither more or less common in the genetics playground, although it may get a few more free lunches.

> **66 Chin fissures such as are found in actors Michael and Kirk Douglas are dominant, but rare (except perhaps in film stars). 99**

The eyes have it

You will find that the topic of dominance causes an irresistible urge in people to discuss eye colour, which they proudly want to cite as a classic example of simple genetic inheritance involving one gene, and a recessive blue and a dominant brown variant. This is a superb opportunity for the bluffer to shine.

Cause doubt by pointing out that if this simple model were true, then people with green eyes wouldn't exist, which they probably wouldn't appreciate very much. Then explain that in reality human eye colour is **polygenic** (*poly* = many) which means it is influenced by many genes.

> **The presence of a single DNA change that alters amino acid number 419 is associated with green or hazel eyes.**

Continue the bluff with some specifics. Declare that the main eye colour gene is thought to be OCA2 (pronounced however you like, so that if someone says it one way, correct them firmly with another) located on chromosome 15, and which makes the creatively named 'P' protein. OCA2 has dozens of possible forms, including blue, green, hazel, brown, and pink alleles. The presence of a single DNA change that alters amino acid number 419 is associated with green or hazel eyes. DNA changes in other locations in OCA2, or in yet other genes such as HERC2 (again pronounce it as you like) might regulate when the P protein is turned on, and can result in blue eyes. Or at least that is one version of the story. The savvy bluffer realises that names of genes and explanations of even simple genetic phenomenon are continuously updated as more information is discovered.

If your audience's eyes start to wander, bring them back by stating authoritatively that in fact most genetic traits involve numerous genes and variants (call them 'multiple alleles' for full effect) which is why geneticists (like you) are ever so clever to sort it out. Even eye colour, you add, must be yet more complicated, since one has to account for hazel, black, velvet-brown, grey, violet blue, ice-blue, steely, or (by this stage) glassy ...

CHANGEABLE GENES

Geneticists are awed and humbled by how well the genetic system works to transmit so much complicated hereditary information from one generation to the next, so you should adopt a similar attitude. Be thankful, but always from the scientific perspective, that mistakes (which you should call 'mutations') do occasionally occur. Without them, there would be no DNA variation. You can get people's attention quite quickly by speculating as to how they would feel should everyone end up looking like, say, former U.S. President Richard Nixon.

> **Be thankful that mistakes (which you should call 'mutations') do occasionally occur.**

There are two basic sources of DNA mutations:

1 External sources, or **mutagens**, which cause DNA damage, such as radiation, certain chemicals and viruses.

2 Spontaneous mutations, which occur by chance in the body as it replicates DNA. (You could draw attention to the fact that due to this effect everyone is born with new mutations, unsettling though that sounds.)

If a mutation occurs in a **somatic** (body) cell, it will not be passed on to the next generation; however, if the DNA alteration occurs in certain genes called oncogenes, cancer and tumours can result. Therefore cancer is actually a disease of the genes, which is why you can say that factors that damage DNA, like cigarettes, sunlight, alcohol, and burnt toast also cause cancer.

66 You could draw attention to the fact that everyone is born with new mutations, unsettling though that sounds. 99

On the other hand, if the change to the DNA occurs while making an egg, sperm or pollen – the **gametes** or **germ** cells (not as in infection, but as in 'the germ of an idea'), the resulting offspring will carry the new DNA sequence in all the cells of its body. This is considered to be the source of genetic variation, which can then be selected during evolution.

Genetics, therefore, suggests an answer to the age-old question: 'Which came first, the chicken or the egg?' The answer, you can dare to say definitively, is the egg. Defend your position with the argument that at some point, there was something that was an 'almost-chicken' bird that laid eggs. In your scenario, one of the eggs had a mutation in its DNA that produced the final change needed to transform the almost-chicken into a genuine chicken (which then crossed a road for questionable purposes).

> **66 The answer to the age-old question: 'Which came first, the chicken or the egg?' you can dare to say, definitively, is the egg. 99**

Jumping genes

If you truly want to blow the minds of the uninitiated, you can tell them that there are genes that can jump around and disrupt other genes, 'jumping genes' or, officially, **transposons**. These are small pieces of DNA that can cut themselves out of one region on a chromosome and insert themselves into another. Barbara McClintock received a Nobel Prize for discovering them, and a great many biologists didn't believe her at first either.

> **66 There are genes that can jump around and disrupt other genes. 99**

Temperature sensitive genes

Some mutations are only evident when the heat is turned up. As befits this role, they are called 'temperature sensitive alleles'. Find a handy Siamese cat or Himalayan rabbit to demonstrate.

> **If you were to strap an ice pack to Fluffy or Flopears for a while, their mid-section would turn black.**

Reveal that the coat colour protein is sensitive to temperature so the parts of the body that are cooler, such as the tips of the nose, ears, paws, and tail, are black, whereas parts of the body, such as the mid-section, that are warmer inactivate the coat colour protein so the fur is white. Thus, if you were to strap an ice pack to Fluffy or Flopears for a while, their mid-section would eventually turn black. However, to demonstrate this might be going a tad too far.

GENETIC RELATIONS

Since it changes over time due to mutations, DNA analysis can precisely determine how various species are related to each other and to humans, providing new and surprising insights into the 'tree of life'. In the past, such so-called **phylogenies** were based solely on outward appearances. So, for example, the big, fat, furless semi-aquatic hippopotamus was thought to be the cousin of the big, fat, furless semi-aquatic pig. But DNA evidence suggests instead that hippos are more closely related to whales and dolphins. Another awesome discovery is that the simple sea urchin (which has no head or limbs) is more closely related to humans than are insects (which at least have legs, eyes, and the ability to be bothersome).

> 66 The simple sea urchin (which has no head or limbs) is more closely related to humans than are insects. 99

Genetics also sheds light on how organisms evolved over time. DNA evidence suggests that a single gene is responsible for the contrast between the digits of bats (which have wings) and mice (which do not). Or, that the few percent difference in the genomes of chimps and humans holds the key to intelligence, unless you think your co-workers are quite similar to other primates.

All in the family

Despite their differences, as members of the same species humans are remarkably similar to each other at the DNA level. Announce dramatically that if you take any two random people on the planet, they will share 99.9% of their DNA. This means that if you compared your DNA with, say, Gregor

Mendel's, on average 999 bases would be exactly the same As, Ts, Cs, and Gs, and one would be different. On the other hand, according to recent research, the number of copies of your genes might be quite different, which could explain why Mendel was fascinated by peas, yet you just eat them.

> **You can finger the gracefully named INSIG2 gene should you carry a few extra kilos.**

Make sure to refer to those 1 in 1000 locations in the DNA that differ by single base pairs as SNPs ('snips' – luckily, there is no need to remember the name Single Nucleotide Polymorphisms). And call the DNA segments that differ in number CNVs ('see-en-vees', short for Copy Number Variations).

When CNVs or SNPs involve genes, they can alter observable characteristics such as people's appearance or health. For example, SNPs have been identified that influence traits ranging from people's response to prescription medications, to becoming obese (thus you can finger the gracefully named INSIG2 gene should you carry a few extra kilos).

The end of privacy

Because of SNPs and other variations in genes, people can be uniquely identified by their DNA, and a surprisingly minute amount is needed for a positive identification – there is enough in only a single piece of hair, a spot of dried sperm on clothing (as Bill Clinton discovered), or a bit of dried blood on a knife. In practice, one of the most widespread uses of DNA tests is to establish paternity.

Governments keep a 'bank' of databases so DNA collected at crime scenes or during arrests can be used for future identifications, which makes hiding difficult for criminals. For example, in one case a single rare allele found at a crime scene matched that of a 14-year-old boy who had tangled with the law. This led police to catch not him, but his paternal uncle, a crook who had the misfortune to share the same unusual genetic pattern.

> **Governments keep a 'bank' of databases so DNA collected at crime scenes or during arrests can be used for future identifications.**

Even anonymous sperm donors are no longer secure. One enterprising 15-year-old whose mother knew only his father's date and place of birth, took a swab to his cheek (a common way to collect DNA) and sent it to one of a growing number of on-line genealogy services. It matched his Y chromosome DNA pattern to that of two men with identical sounding, but differently spelled, last names. Guessing his own father had the same last name as these two men, the son did more web sleuthing. Within a mere 10 days, he had successfully tracked down his 'anonymous' father.

This ability to identify people leads to some provocative privacy issues such as:

- Should employers and insurance agencies have access to people's DNA records (or that of their incarcerated relatives for that matter)?

- If people are tested and defective genes found, should their family members be informed, since they are also at risk?

But the end of privacy has potential advantages. In the future, you may be able to grab a piece of hair from someone you fancy, get it tested, and receive his or her DNA profile. This may tell you about an individual's vulnerability to certain diseases, or propensity for various behaviours such as snoring or smoking in bed, saving you the bother of future dates if the results are not to your liking. (Although it should be kept in mind that others could do the same to you.)

❝A DNA profile may tell you about an individual's propensity for various behaviours such as snoring or smoking in bed. ❞

Reading human history

Small variations in DNA also hold important clues about the history of the human race. For example, research suggests that even after they separated into two species 6 million years ago, human and chimp ancestors might have bred with each other (leading one to inevitable comparisons with the spousal choices of certain friends).

DNA research also supports fossil evidence that mankind originally arose on the African continent, which you should call the Out-of-Africa Theory. One study (deemed statistically unsubstantiated, but still widely cited) even suggested that humans were all descended from a single female living in Africa 150,000 years ago, who researchers rather aptly named 'Eve'.

66 One study suggested that humans were all descended from a single female living in Africa 150,000 years ago. 99

Similar studies shed light on the mystery of what happened to the Neanderthals. These large brawny primates co-existed with humans in Europe 29,000 years ago, then just 'disappeared'. Conflicting theories suggested that they were absorbed by interbreeding with human ancestors, or else that the human species killed them off. DNA extracted from the ribs of a Neanderthal infant buried in southern Russia suggests that the extinction theory is more accurate, since no remnants of Neanderthal DNA have been found in modern humans. (On the other hand, a quick look at the hefty linemen in American football teams seems to provide convincing evidence to the contrary.)

Genghis Khan's kin

Analysis of Y chromosome DNA suggests that the 13th-century Mongolian warrior Genghis Khan may have achieved more during his lifetime than ruling the largest empire in the world. It seems a whopping 8% of men living in the former Mongol region (roughly 16 million, or half a percent of the world's male population) sport nearly identical Y-chromosomes. This suggests that they are all descendants of the same man, presumably the great Khan. Make sure to propound this theory as authoritatively as possible, even though there are other explanations, such as there being some advantage conferred by this particular Y-chromosome that helped it spread so widely. The speculation is neither easily confirmed nor refuted without discovering the grave of Genghis Khan himself and extracting his DNA (which, to put it in perspective, is less likely than finding your plain black umbrella left behind on a bus last week).

> **Discovering the grave of Genghis Khan and extracting his DNA is less likely than finding the plain black umbrella you left on a bus last week.**

It is often supposed that people with similar surnames share common ancestors. To test this theory, celebrity geneticist Bryan Sykes, a professor at the University of Oxford, looked at DNA samples from 61 male volunteers who shared his surname. He found that half the group were related to him since they shared four distinctive regions of the Y-chromosome with his. The other half did not, suggesting some degree of infidelity in the Sykes ancestors. In separate work, he discovered evidence that modern Europeans are descended from one of seven 'clan mothers' who lived at different times during the Ice Age, whom he calls the 'seven daughters of Eve'.

ENGINEERING GENES

The ability to move genes from one species to another has made possible organisms that are 'transgenic', 'genetically engineered', or 'genetically modified' (your choice). More pragmatic examples of genetically modified organisms (GMO) include goats engineered with human genes so that they produce human proteins in their milk for use as drugs to treat diseases. This

> **Genetically modified organisms include goats engineered so they produce human proteins in their milk.**

technology has also been used for such debatable purposes as Alba, a bio-luminescent rabbit created in 2000 for an American conceptual artist as a creative statement and future personal playmate. Alba was made by the insertion of a jellyfish gene, the Green Fluorescent Protein (GFP). When exposed to ultraviolet 'black' lights, the otherwise white-furred Alba emitted an eerie green glow. This stirred an international flurry of debate over whether it was ethically right to create a genetically modified animal purely for entertainment (although to be fair, the same could be said of Teacup Poodles, which serve no apparent practical purpose). An emotional custody battle ensued when the French lab that created Alba refused to turn the rabbit over to the artist to become his family pet.

> **66 When exposed to ultraviolet 'black' lights, white-furred Alba emitted an eerie green glow. 99**

There are also such things as Gene Knockouts. Do not be deterred by the news that these are experiments where a gene is removed to observe the effect on the viability of the organism. Let the phrase have the space that it so richly deserves: we do all know some gene knockouts, after all.

Genetically modified crops

The most widespread commercial use for transgenic technology is in the area of genetically modified crops, where additional genes such as pesticide resistance are inserted to improve yields. Other efforts include altering foods like rice to produce critical nutrients such as Vitamin A, bananas to contain vaccines against infectious diseases such as hepatitis B, or sweet potatoes to resist a deadly African virus. It has also been possible to engineer farmed fish to mature more quickly, and for pigs to produce pork with more of the 'good' type of omega 3 fats (which is happy news for bacon lovers everywhere).

> **❝ The worry is that parents will try to engineer children with good looks, intelligence or Schwarzenegger pecs. ❞**

Of course GM foods are a hotly debated topic so it's worth calling attention to the fact that, despite concern over the technology, it is estimated that around 70% of processed foods, ranging from croissants to corn oil and any food with soy in it, contain genetically modified ingredients.

Designer babies

People love to bring up the issue of designer babies, and will hold strong views about whether scientists should be allowed to design children at will by picking out what genes they will have. The worry is that parents will try to engineer children with certain desirable characteristics, such as good looks, intelligence, or Schwarzenegger pecs.

Bluffers can put such fears to rest with the simple statement "Not before pigs fly". Science in this case is leagues behind the imagination. To illustrate, remind your listener that even something as simple as eye colour involves multiple genes, so it is

> **For an impressive starting gambit, tell your audience that they have almost certainly met a clone.**

a bit naïve to think that geneticists can understand what genes do well enough to get anywhere near designing babies with complicated traits like intelligence or personality.

At least until they figure out how to equip hogs with wings. Feel free to add that in any case, people have been making designer offspring of sorts for thousands of years, every time they choose a mate.

Cloning

Few subjects in genetics have captured the popular imagination as has cloning, or sparked such fierce dissent between otherwise peaceable and well-mannered friends or family members. The best tactic is to start the conversation with some science before wading in, as most opinions are ill-informed in any case.

For an impressive starting gambit, tell your audience that they have almost certainly already met a clone. When they protest, point out that while cloning is sometimes considered the exclusive province of cutting edge research and film noir, there are actually human clones already – in the form of identical twins.

They will also have eaten some. Nature itself has been successfully cloning plants for billions of years, sometimes with delicious results. For example, when a strawberry plant sends out a form of modified stem called a runner, a new plant can arise from it that is genetically identical to the first plant.

Parthenogenesis

If you want to stun your audience, tell them that plants are not the only organisms that can clone themselves naturally, and then mention **parthenogenesis**, the process whereby (under certain conditions) the unfertilised eggs of some animals including certain types of small invertebrates, worms, fish, lizards, frogs and even sharks can develop into full-grown adults that are clones of the females that laid the eggs. There is even the strange case of the Wolbachia parasitic bacteria family, which can turn their female insect hosts parthenogenic in order to enhance their own propagation. It seems that in all these cases males are quite unnecessary – an unsettling thought for some.

❝ It seems that parthenogenesis can make males unnecessary, an unsettling thought for some. ❞

Of course, this is not what all the fuss and excitement is about, so bring the conversation quickly to the topic of 'reproductive cloning', which is the term used to describe attempts to create new animal life through cloning. To succeed in this topic, you will need to be intimately (in the intellectual sense) familiar with Dolly the sheep, the first mammal to be cloned from an adult cell.

Dolly

Quite an attractive ewe, Dolly gained phenomenal worldwide attention after she was born at the Roslin Institute in Scotland in July 1996, cloned by Ian Wilmut and his cronies.

Dolly was formed by taking the genetic material from a mammary (breast) gland cell of an adult Finn Dorsett sheep, and putting it into the egg of a Scottish blackface ewe. Since the entire nucleus was moved, call this 'the nuclear transfer technique' for added pizzaz. The lamb, Dolly, was an exact genetic replica of the adult female Finn Dorsett sheep who donated the genes to the egg, not the ewe who gave birth to her. For levity, remind your listeners that that this woolly farm animal was named after Dolly Parton, the country and western singer who sports her own set of impressive mammary glands.

> **66 This woolly farm animal was named after Dolly Parton, the country and western singer who sports her own set of impressive mammary glands. 99**

52

Following Dolly, modifications of the technique have been used to produce cloned mammals of many types, including cows, pigs, goats, monkeys and mice. The first cloned kitten was named 'CC' (short for Carbon Copy) and was born in 2001 to scientists in Texas. The

> **66 The first cloned kitten was named 'CC' (short for Carbon Copy). 99**

efforts were funded in part by the Missyplicity Project, which aimed to create clones of a mixed-breed dog named Missy.

Now there are even companies that will (for a not inconsiderable fee) make an exact genetic replica of your favourite pet, or bank its DNA for future cloning possibilities, should you so desire. For those who can cough up the dough, a warning is given that the new Fluffy or Fang probably won't be exactly like the original ones, due to the nature/nurture effect.

> **66 Now there are even companies that will (for a not inconsiderable fee) make an exact genetic replica of your favourite pet. 99**

Nor are long-term prospects guaranteed. Dolly seemed to lead a healthy life, except that she died early, at the age of 6, raising questions about whether this was due to being a clone, or a result of the type of tragic bad luck that seems to befall celebrities of all species.

Cloning people

You will undoubtedly find that people's biggest interest in the subject of cloning is the possibility of making exact genetic copies of humans, such as themselves. The topic brings up a mind-boggling array of philosophical, ethical and legal questions about the nature of life itself. Don't hesitate to raise such knotty issues as to whether:

- a clone should have the same rights as the original person;
- it is right for a family to re-create a child lost in an accident;
- it would be reasonable for infants cloned from adults to see their future (for better or worse).

Rest assured that at present these are all theoretical questions, so there is no correct answer, other than your own. And don't hesitate to poke fun at the many fraudulent claims of success in cloning humans, such as those by Korean scientists in 2005. But if you want to exit the tangled debate, you can always memorise and recite this little ditty:

Mary had a little lamb,
its fleece was slightly grey
It didn't have a father,
just some borrowed DNA.

It sort of had a mother,
though the ovum was on loan;
'Twas not so much a lambkin,
as a little lamby clone.

And soon it had a fellow clone,
and soon it had some more;
They followed her to school one day,
all cramming through the door;
It made the children laugh and sing,
the teachers found it droll
There were too many lamby clones,
for Mary to control.

No other could control the sheep,
their programmes didn't vary
So scientists resolved it all –
by simply cloning Mary.

Stem cells

To continue bluffing convincingly on the subject, state that geneticists have a broader definition of the term cloning, which includes any process that results in exact genetic replicas, whether it be a whole new organism (such as Dolly), or simply more copies of genes or parts of organisms such as cells and organs. For example, the field of thera-peutic cloning aims to replace defective cells or organs with healthy ones. This approach is often less controversial than reproductive cloning because the goal is to help cure maladies, rather than create an entirely new person who will carry with them their own personality and potentially arguable privileges such as taxes, death and dieting.

> **Although no-one is close to being able to repair worn-out cynical old brains, the technique could potentially be applied to diseases.**

Although no-one is close to being able to repair worn-out cynical old brains, the technique could potentially be applied to diseases such as cancer, Parkinson's, spinal cord injuries and diabetes. The advantage of therapeutic cloning over more traditional organ transplants is that the cells are genetically similar to the patient's, reducing chances of rejection (biological, not emotional).

> **Stem cells are those whose job in the body is to make other, more specialised cells.**

One category of cells in particular, stem cells, is especially amenable to therapeutic cloning (and to controversy). Stem cells are those whose job in the body is to make other, more specialised cells. They are found in embryos, and in the organs and tissues of adults where their job is to replace cells as needed. Every cell in the body 'stems' from this type of cell. Like actors looking for a script to determine their character, stem cells wait for signals to instruct them what type of cell to become (except, unlike would-be thespians, their odds of success are fairly decent).

The two categories of stem cells, adult and embryonic, are quite different from each other. Embryonic stem cells are 'pluripotent', meaning that they can give rise to all the cells in the body and therefore can be used to replace any cells that have been damaged or destroyed. Although embryonic stem cells have proved valuable, fierce controversy surrounds their use, due to ethical questions about the 'personhood' of their source. (Arguments on this topic cannot be won, so are best avoided.)

> **"Asking blood stem cells to regenerate heart or liver or brain is like asking comedian Jerry Lewis to play Shakespeare."**

Adult stem cells, on the other hand, are less controversial, but can differentiate only into cell types similar to their organ or tissue of origin and hence are considered multi-potent. For example, asking blood stem cells to regenerate heart or liver or brain is like asking comedian Jerry Lewis to play Shakespeare – it betrays their intrinsic nature. At least, that's how things stand at the moment, but there are many scientific efforts underway to increase the repertoire of the Jerry Lewises of the body.

GENETIC RESEARCH

Classical geneticists spend a great deal of time mating various organisms and seeing if they can predict what their offspring are likely to look like.

Since humans prove to be such cranky subjects, for many types of genetic research scientists must look elsewhere to decipher inheritance. They pick species which you should call 'animal models' or 'model systems', that lend themselves well to studies in genetics, such as the pea and the fruit fly. It is not that they are so terribly fascinated with peas and fruit flies, but rather that the peas and flies have a life cycle of a few weeks, thousands can be kept in the lab for very low cost, and they have similarities (at least from a genetics' perspective) to humans.

> **It is not that they are so terribly fascinated with peas and fruit flies, but rather that the peas and flies have a life cycle of a few weeks.**

There are few things more effective for bluffing than throwing out a few Latin terms. They succeed where many others do not. Therefore, discussing the merits of the following species could come in handy:

- **Mice**. Geneticists tend to think of mice as if they were tiny furry humans since, as mammals, they have so many similar traits and thus are helpful for understanding a wide variety of human diseases. Next time a guest finds a mouse scurrying about in your house, assure them that you are using *Mus domesticus* (muss doe-mess-ti-kuss) for an important genetics study. Then, when they aren't looking, go out and get yourself a decent cat to manage the experiment.

- **Fruit flies** – These are the irritating active specks you find congregating around your bananas if you leave them out too long. Tell people that their presence is not due to your sloppy cleaning habits, but rather you are conducting an experiment using *Drosophila melanogaster* (drow-soff-i-lah mell-ann-oh-gass-ter).

- **Worms**. Not the big juicy ones that birds go for, but tiny ones about a millimetre in length that look like specks of dust. You can point at virtually any soil anywhere and confidently predict that nematodes are squirming happily away in it, perhaps some that are of the species *Caenorhabditis elegans* (seen-or-abb-die-tiss-elegance'). With fewer than 1,000 cells, they mature in a fleeting three days.

> **66 With fewer than 1,000 cells, they mature in a fleeting three days. 99**

- **Yeast**. Besides being crucial to two of humankind's greatest culinary treats – bread and beer – yeast is a convenient model for geneticists since it is only one cell big. You could show real sophistication next time you order a beer by asking for the beverage made by *Saccharomyces cerevisiae* (sack-or-oh-my-sees sera-viss-see-ay), but this could well get you kicked out of the bar.

- **Bacteria**. These are the bugs that live in your gut and digest food if you fail to, and sometimes make you sick if you have the wrong ones. The type geneticists use most often is the notorious *Escherichia coli* which fortunately scientists only ever refer to in conversation by its nickname E. coli (ee coal-eye).

In case you are asked, be prepared to acknowledge that geneticists use a variety of other species as well. For example, the genetics and genomes of dogs are studied because they have over 35 diseases in common with people, there are dozens of well-defined breeds, and they make wonderful pets before, during and after the studies. They also can shake paws, herd sheep, and become obsessive, all interesting behaviours to understand from a genetics perspective. But you would simply sound foolish if you called your lovable, furry friends by their Latin name *Canis lupus familiaris*,

66 The genetics and genomes of dogs are studied because they have over 35 diseases in common with people. **99**

so you can just stick with 'dog' as in "Yes, this is my wonderful wuckums, smoochy-poochy-poo".

Peas please

As the progenitor of genetics, it is essential that you are able to discuss Mendel and his experiments with garden peas, even if the vegetable is not to your liking and you think they are often overcooked. If you can think of nothing else to say, draw attention to the fact that the great Mendel ended up as a monk called Brother Gregor because he couldn't pass the university exams when trying to get his teaching credentials.

It is a point in his favour that unlike many famous discoveries Mendel's did not rely on any advancement in technology. Instead, he chose

> **" The great Mendel ended up as a monk called Brother Gregor because he couldn't pass the university exams. "**

simple materials, and was methodical in his experiments. Since his experiments involved examining tens of thousands of plants, one can also applaud his patience.

Most people know that he studied garden peas, but you can impress even seasoned geneticists by enthusing about the reasons why he chose them: peas were cheap (cheap is always good, especially when you're a monk) and many varieties of true-breeding (that is, pure-breeding) ones were available. Better yet, pea plants have both male and female sexual organs. This meant that Mendel could practise **selfing** (breeding them with themselves). Or he could breed them with each other by delicately snipping off the male parts (ouch!) and individually moving the pollen to other plants.

> **66** Whenever there is something you cannot explain, you can simply smile knowingly and call it "non-Mendelian inheritance". **99**

Be sure to marvel that Mendel was either exceedingly brilliant, or outstandingly lucky (pick either one since it is a matter of debate) in choosing seven straightforward traits – such as pea colour (yellow and green), pea shape (round and wrinkled), flower colour, flower position, stem length, pod shape, and pod colour – that:

- were controlled by only one gene,
- were fully dominant or recessive, and
- did not interact with other genes or the environment.

Most genetics is far trickier than this, which turns out to be extremely convenient for bluffers. It means that whenever there is something you cannot explain, you can simply smile knowingly and call it "non-Mendelian inheritance". This works in most situations, except of course when discussing the genetics of someone's nose, in which case you should agree that it looks like whichever parent, movie star, or celeb they claim it does, and leave it at that.

Or you can bring up the question of whether or not Mendel faked his results. Some statistical analyses suggest that his data were too good to be real and must have been rounded off. (An important lesson here for bluffers: if you fudge, but turn out to be correct in your science, you are often forgiven.)

Three to one

If you hate arithmetic or statistics, there is a handy trick to handling the topic. Simply respond to any question with "The ratio is 3 to 1". That's it. In the last example, for instance, you would reveal that the ratio of yellow to green peas is 3 to 1 (which geneticists write as 3:1). It's a phrase that always sounds decisive, even when it is wrong. You can wax eloquent about the fact that Mendel was able to deduce much about the existence of genes based on the 3 to 1 ratio.

> **If you hate arithmetic or statistics, there is a handy trick: simply respond to any question with 'The ratio is 3 to 1'.**

For all seven traits he studied, when he bred the true breeding peas (call them the parental generation), the resulting first generation (call them F1 pronounced 'eff-one' for first filial) all looked like the dominant version. When he then crossed (mated) the F1s with each other, the next generation, F2, all had the 3 to 1 ratio of dominant to recessive.

This phrase is especially helpful when referring to cases in which only one gene or trait is involved, called 'monohybrid' crosses, such as between some-one who has dimples, and some-one who does not. Be forewarned that the ratios start to get more complicated when two genes are involved, called 'dihybrid' crosses. This would be the case in humans for eye colour, where the 'bey2' and 'gey' genes are both involved. If at all possible, make every effort to avoid discussion of dihybrid crosses, since they quickly get more dense with F2 ratios like 9:3:3:1. However, if challenged, you can always say that for each individual trait "the expected ratio is 3 to 1".

> **❝ For some reason, humans do not want to mate with another individual just so that a geneticist can see how their children will turn out. ❞**

HUMAN GENETICS

In many ways, humans have proved a terribly diffi-cult species for geneticists to study. For some reason, they do not want to mate with another individual just so that a geneticist can see how their children will turn out. Unlike pea plants, humans tend to be quite testy about having parts of their reproductive organs snipped off. Never mind that even if humans co-operated, a single experiment would take several decades to complete while the paltry few children (by pea or fruit fly standards) grew up, which is a long time even for the pace of science.

> **Unlike pea plants, humans tend to be quite testy about having parts of their reproductive organs snipped off.**

You can caution that because of this there are still many aspects of human genetics (and their mating behaviour for that matter) that have yet to be solved. This turns out to be extremely handy when you are inevitably asked questions about someone's own family. People will love telling you about their Uncle Bob or their second cousin once removed who had some odd trait, such as a tendency to rock back and forth while talking, or exceptionally sweaty feet.

> **People will love telling you about their Uncle Bob who had some odd trait, such as a tendency to rock back and forth while talking.**

To dispense with such enquiries, simply state "No" decisively if it is an undesirable trait and "Yes" if it is a preferred one. If they persist in asking why, say you would be happy to answer if they agree to breed with someone of your choosing.

Pedigrees

Scientists who focus on human genetics spend a great deal of time drawing family trees (in expert nomenclature 'pedigrees'). If your listeners find it humorous that the term is more commonly applied to charting the bloodlines of purebred dogs and race horses, tease them that far more is probably known about the typical pet pooch's ancestry than their own. Pedigrees sound straightforward, but humans,

> **An obsession with the bagpipes might be more common in a family that originates from Scotland, but it is unlikely to be genetic.**

as is their wont, tend to complicate matters. These include falsehoods about real parentage, multiple marriages, and worst of all (if a geneticist is researching a trait), incomplete family histories. Add to this the harsh truth that most traits involve complex interactions between genes and the environment, as well as just plain random chance, and geneticists do what all self-respecting scientists do: assign obscure terms to the phenomenon. You should be quite happy with this situation, as it makes your efforts ever so much easier.

When traits show up more strongly in some individuals than others even with the same genes and environmental conditions, you will call it 'variable expressivity'. Explain that the situation is similar to the variable expressivity seen in the brown and black spots of Beagle dogs, which are bigger in some, and smaller in others, even when they have the same gene combinations.

If you feel expansive, add that even when the gene variants are present, sometimes they don't show up at all. Call this 'incomplete penetrance'. This can prove quite handy when meeting potential mates: assure them that you have the genetics for brains, beauty and brawn, but that "they failed to fully manifest in you due to the genes' incomplete penetrance".

Diseases

Conveniently for bluffers, just because something is more common in a family, does not mean it is genetic. For example, an obsession with the bagpipes might be more common in a family that originates from Scotland, but it is unlikely to be genetic (at least one hopes not).

Your audience will be glad to know that there are quite a few human diseases – e.g, albinism (no skin or hair pigments) and achondroplasia (dwarfism) – for which the genetics is well understood because they:

- have straightforward inheritance patterns;
- are caused by single genes; and
- are usually fully dominant or recessive.

Be sure to say that much less is known about factors involved in many common afflictions like diabetes, heart disease, cancer and obesity. In complex disorders like these, not only can there can be an inherited predisposition for the disease due to interactions of multiple genes, but symptoms are also influenced by the environment. For example, some people have a genetic tendency for heart disease, but it would be less of an issue if so many riveting game shows did not tempt them to sit glued to the television all day.

Population genetics

Because sorting out the genetics of individuals can be so complicated geneticists have a handy way of ignoring it and looking at large groups of people instead. Call this approach 'population genetics' and explain that the group in question can range from a particular race or ethnic group, to those residing in an entire continent.

> **Because sorting out the genetics of individuals can be so complicated geneticists have a handy way of ignoring it.**

The approach involves first calculating the population's gene frequencies, or how common certain traits are in that group. The goal then is to compare the gene frequencies between the groups, and determine how they change over time and place. For example, blond hair tends to be more common (frequent) in Northern Europe than, say, Southern Europe. (Note: we are speaking of real blond hair – not the kind that comes from a bottle.)

The next question geneticists ask is why there are differences. Rest assured that there are only two basic answers to this question:

1 **Drift**. It could just be pure chance (but call it drift, like a log drifting aimlessly on the ocean) that caused a gene variant to become more common in some groups than others. For example, it could be that more of the ancestors of Northern Europeans happened to have blond hair for no reason other than chance.

2 **Selection**. Sometimes a gene is more common, or becomes more common, because it is selected, in the sense that those who have it have more offspring, thus making it more prevalent

> **Perhaps blond hair conferred advantages by allowing more absorption of the sun's rays.**

in the population: e.g., perhaps blond hair conferred advantages by allowing more absorption of the sun's rays (more limited in the North) to produce sufficient Vitamin D.

Conveniently, it's almost impossible to tell the difference between the two possibilities. This means you can plump for either in any situation with the utmost assurance. (The only exception is if you are talking about someone's ancestors, in which case you may opt to emphasise selection.)

66 If the subject of Hardy Weinberg equilibrium arises, don't lose your balance. 99

One example you can give where selection is thought to have played a role in human evolution is the ability to digest the sugar lactose in milk as adults. Except for Europeans, most of the world's population cannot eat dairy foods like ice cream after childhood without getting appalling stomach aches. It is thought that sometime within the last 10,000 years Europeans acquired the variant (a single change in DNA located in the regulatory region of the lactase gene that encodes the information to make the lactase enzyme that digests milk sugar). The variant presumably conferred an advantage, and so spread, as dependence on domesticated dairy animals became more prevalent in Europe.

If the subject of Hardy Weinberg equilibrium arises, don't lose your balance. Rest assured that it hardly ever exists. Theoretically (and you know how well that corresponds to reality), you can predict the genotypes in the population by minding your 'ps and qs' – that is, the ps being the more common allele, and the qs the less common. Airily dismiss the entire topic with the claim that it assumes such things as that all members of the population produce the same number of offspring, which, for perspective, is as unlikely as remaining upright after not minding your ps and qs at the bar.

The measure of genes

You can observe that all the genes that Mendel studied had 'distinct states': the pea was either smooth or wrinkled, yellow or green, and you ate it or you didn't. In real life, there are many inherited characteristics that vary along a continuum which you can explain are types of 'continuous variation' – such as hair colour, skin tone, or leg and arm hairiness.

Some continuous characteristics are easily measured. If so, call them 'quantitative traits'. Height is the usual example given here. People are not always exactly five feet (1.75m) tall or six feet (2m) tall, but vary along a continuum that is easily quantified (as well as generally exaggerated by those who consider themselves at the shorter end).

> **66 The pea was either smooth or wrinkled, yellow or green, and you ate it or you didn't. 99**

Fitness

You can also introduce the concept of fitness, which means rather more than how often someone lifts weights at the gym. For geneticists, fitness is a measurement of how well an organism is likely to survive in its environment and have offspring. The more fit it is, the better able it will be to reproduce.

> **Though humans have 23 pairs, ants have only one pair, dogs 39 pairs, and crayfish 100 pairs.**

Charles Darwin's theory of evolution can be understood from a population genetics perspective. Traits that increase an organism's fitness tend to increase in frequency because individuals who possess them have more offspring, a process he called natural selection. Evolution has been well established and confirmed through DNA evidence too, except for people who espouse certain religious beliefs, in which case this whole process may not exist at all.

BUDDY CHROMOSOMES

People's chromosomes come in pairs, which means that humans are **diploid** (*di* for two). For added dazzle, call the pairs **homologues** and casually remark that, though humans have 23, other species don't. Ants have only one pair, dogs 39 pairs, and crayfish 100 pairs.

The sperm and eggs of humans have only one

copy of each pair (the one that will get passed on to the child), so geneticists call them **haploid**.

In humans and most animals the possession of extra sets of chromosomes typically results in death, though in many plants it results in bigger fruit which is infinitely preferable. Favourites include bananas (triploid with three sets) bread wheat (hexaploid or six sets) and strawberries (octaploid or eight sets).

66 There are more bacteria cells in one person's gut than there are humans on the planet. **99**

Not all chromosomes come in pairs, nor are they linear. The one that bacteria have is circular, which seems to work quite well for them considering that there are more bacteria cells in one person's gut than there are humans on the planet.

Mighty mitochondria

An amusing party game is to bet on how much DNA people have in their chromosomes. Make sure to wager decent amounts of cash, since:

a the DNA from a single cell is about as long as a person is tall;
b if you took all the DNA in all the cells of a person's body and laid them end to end, they would go to the moon and back, not just once, not twice, but thousands of times. (But don't try this at home.)

You can inject an element of surprise by explaining that not all DNA is contained in the 23 pairs of linear chromosomes. Assure your bluffees they also have another set of chromosomes that are composed of circular DNA. These are located in the hundreds of mitochondria in each cell that are required for turning food into energy.

❝ Explain, if asked, that mitochondria were once a bunch of hitchhiking bacteria that decided never to leave the cell. ❞

If anyone asks why they bother to have their own DNA, you can explain that mitochondria were once a bunch of hitchhiking bacteria that decided never to leave the cell.

For a final touch, make sure to mention that people only inherit mitochondria and their DNA from their mothers, since eggs are stuffed with them, while the sperm transfers none to the egg. This 'matriarchal inheritance' has proved helpful for DNA studies tracing relationships between races and species because there is no pesky reshuffling of genes between the sexes to worry about.

Sex chromosomes

Most people spend a great deal of time thinking about sex, and geneticists are no different. They just try to pretend they're not by talking about it in terms of chromosomes. In humans, one's gender is determined by the X and Y factor, the 23rd pair of chromosomes. Women have a double X (XX), while men have one of each, so they are XY.

Since XXs are all that women have, they can only pass on the 'X factor' to their children, so in order to produce a male the egg has to receive a Y chromosome from the father. The fact that this leads to the conclusion that men determine the sex of the child is perhaps best saved for marital spats in which one parent must be blamed for something in order to provide temporary psychological relief to the other.

> **The fact that this leads to the conclusion that men determine the sex of the child is perhaps best saved for marital spats in which one parent must be blamed for something.**

Not all species determine sex this same way. In the bird world, it's the males that have two of the same chromosome (ZZ), while females have two different sex chromosomes (ZW). However, it's probably useless to mention this in relation to a marital spat between poultry pairs, unless it pertains to their reasons for crossing the road.

Sex linkage

Genes that are located on the X or Y chromosome are called 'sex linked' (a term that is guaranteed to perk up the dullest conversation) and they have peculiar characteristics. Women have two copies of each gene on the X chromosome, whereas men only have one. This means that men must inherit only one copy of a recessive trait to show it, whereas women must receive two.

> **Red–green colour-blindness occurs in fewer than 1 in 400 women.**

Assert that about 1 in 20 men cannot tell the difference between certain shades of red and green because a gene on their X chromosome responsible for detecting light is altered. But red–green colour-blindness occurs in fewer than 1 in 400 women because even if they inherit the recessive defective gene on an X from one parent, they usually get the dominant functional variant on the other.

But you can also point out that the X chromosome contains a lot of genes on it, most of which are not related to sex. The Y chromosome, on the other hand, is much smaller, and does not contain as many genes. You should not make jokes about how few genes men have on their Y chromosome as they will not usually appreciate it.

> **You should not make jokes about how few genes men have on their Y chromosome as they will not usually appreciate it.**

You can tell them that some of the very few genes on the Y chromosome are responsible for starting the process of making the recipient of the chromosome develop testes rather than ovaries. The testes in turn churn out a hormone, testosterone, at high levels, that causes other characteristic male attributes, like an inability to ask for directions and the tendency to enjoy going fishing.

Inactivating Xs

One odd consequence of women having twice the number of X chromosomes as men is that in a bizarre scheme to compensate, female mammals randomly condense one X chromosome in each cell into a dense mass called a **Barr body**. This shuts down all the genes on that chromosome in a process called **X inactivation**, and results in equalisation between the sexes (at a chromosomal level at least; salaries have yet to catch up).

If you see a tortoiseshell – or calico – cat (one with patches of orange, black and white), confidently announce that it is sure to be a female because a

> **If you see a tortoiseshell – or calico – cat (one with patches of orange, black and white), confidently announce that it is likely to be a female.**

coat colour gene on the X chromosome has the orange allele off in some patches, and the black off in others (the white is due to an entirely different gene that causes spotting). You can consider this a case of cat inactivation that bars their bodies from anything other than excessive napping.

Altered chromosomes

People often have trouble remembering where their shoes are, so imagine trying to keep track of 23 pairs of shoes that move about by themselves and that all look similar, and you will have some empathy for what a human cell must do to organise all its chromosomes.

❝Imagine trying to keep track of 23 pairs of shoes that move about by themselves and all look similar.❞

Most of the time the cell does a remarkable job of this, but occasionally mistakes happen and a new cell doesn't receive one of the chromosomes, or acquires an extra one – a process called 'nondisjunction'. Humans almost never make it to adulthood if they do not possess the right number of chromosomes in their cells (though one major exception is Down Syndrome, which results from trisomy 21, or three copies of the smallest chromosome).

There can also be alterations to the chromosomes themselves, where bits are deleted, duplicated, or inverted. There are even cases where parts of one chromosome are reattached to another chromosome, an occurrence called 'translocation' (not like moving home with your significant other; more like splitting up with a partner then dating someone worse).

Problems in chromosomes can be checked through **karyotypes** (carry-oh-types), a procedure in which chromosomes are dressed in their finest outfits (i.e. stained with dye*), then made to pose in a row from biggest to smallest, then photographed through a microscope (all the genes smile and say 'allele'). The ultimate family portrait.

TOPICS TO AVOID

Any conversation about genetics lasting longer than seven and a half minutes will inevitably bring up a number of issues that can quickly dissolve your well-planned spiel into a seething debate. It cannot be emphasised enough that if you wish to master the art of bluffing in genetics and keep your limbs intact, you will steer the conversation

> **❝ If you wish to master the art of bluffing in genetics and keep your limbs intact, you will steer the conversation away from these matters. ❞**

as quickly as possible away from these matters, and on to safer ground. Topics to avoid in all circumstances include the influence of genetics on:

– Intelligence (such as IQ or lack thereof)
– Personality (such as shyness or obnoxiousness)

* Indeed the very name chromosome means coloured cells as in *chroma* from the Greek meaning 'colour' and *soma* from the Greek meaning 'body'.

- Race (such as propensities for disease)
- Sexual preference (such as foot fetishes)
- Mental illness (such as depression, author's block or playing Aussie Rules football)
- Addiction (such as alcohol, drugs or bargain shopping)
- Differences between men and women (such as scientific acuity, or ability to ask directions).

Scientists are cautious about expressing opinions on such subjects, and news bulletins in these areas are hardly issued before they are retracted, refuted, changed or modified. Even if reports come from top universities, they are still highly controversial. They are also subjects about which people form very strong sentiments, so facts tend to be selectively pulled out to support or refute personal beliefs.

66 You may happily enquire whether or not the results of certain findings have been validated – a ploy that gently implies that judgement should be withheld until they are. 99

You would be wise, when these topics arise, to prepare a one-size-fits-all rejoinder. The terms 'validation' or 'confirmed' are extremely useful here. Scientists will always try to repeat or replicate experiments in order to make sure they are correct. Therefore you may happily enquire whether or not the results of certain findings have been validated –

a ploy that gently implies that judgement should be withheld until they are. You are pretty safe because they rarely have, which is why they are so hotly debated and usually later retracted.

Then steer the conversation to safer ground with phrases such as, "Did you know that even eye colour is not only polygenic, but involves epistastis and multiple alleles?" Be assured that the success of this diversionary tactic has been well validated by experienced geneticists.

> **People who actively seek out excitement and risky activities, such as hang gliding, or wrestling crocodiles, can attribute some of their behaviour to genetics.**

If you cannot resist venturing into these topics, try throwing out some interesting, but more firmly established nuggets yourself (though if anyone else brings them up, be sure to question their validity.)

Risk taking: People who actively seek out excitement and risky activities, such as driving fast cars, hang gliding, or wrestling crocodiles, can attribute some of their behaviour to genetics. Folks who score high for novelty-seeking in personality profiles are more likely to have DNA alterations in the DRD4 (or Dopamine Receptor D4) gene that is involved in the regulation of dopamine, a chemical in the brain that has been linked to risk-taking.

Bitter revenge: At last, a decent excuse for hating certain vegetables, like broccoli and Brussels sprouts – one can blame it on genes. For some people the bitter chemical in these greens is more pronounced than in others. A change in a few bits of DNA on chromosome 7 results in the difference between tasters.

Drugs: One gene, CYP2D6, is needed to process about a fifth of all commonly used medical drugs. This gene varies between individuals, resulting in their having different reactions to drugs, such as codeine. About 1% of Asian people and 10% of Caucasians are completely absent in this gene, which means that people from different ethnic groups have different probabilities of responding to certain drugs. But of course it's individuals, not statistics, who swallow the pills.

> **“It has been discovered that changes in a gene located on chromosome 2 called 'hPer2' can alter one's internal clock.”**

Morning larks: Good news for those who struggle to wake up to the morning alarm, or have the opposite problem – fall asleep at 7p.m. and wake around 2 a.m. It has been discovered that changes in a gene located on chromosome 2 called 'hPer2' can alter one's internal clock. There's nothing like being able to blame your genes for tardy time-keeping.

GLOSSARY

Allele One of a number of alternate forms of a gene. If there were a gene for genetics, it could have the 'bluffers' allele', and the 'non-bluffers' allele'.

Bases Basic building blocks of DNA (also called nucleotides). Origin of the term 'cover all your bases' meaning to keep your DNA secret.

Carriers People who can transmit a recessive disorder to their offspring, but do not have the disorder themselves. A carrier is what your spouse is for every undesirable trait in your children that certainly didn't come from you.

Cell Basic building block or unit of all life, usually containing a complete set of the organism's DNA. Useful for imprisoning genes.

Chromosome How the cell packages genes, consisting of a single long strand of DNA wound around proteins. Without chromosomes, the two metres of DNA in each cell would be hopelessly tangled, resulting in something more like spaghetti than inheritance.

Cloning Taking the genetic material from one organism to make another entity identical to the first. Would eliminate the need for actually going on dates.

Cross Mating of plants or animals for genetics experiments, but not for fun. How geneticists feel when experiments don't work as planned.

Diploid Organism with two copies of each chromosome. One of each pair is from your mother, and one is from your father, unless you're a clone, in which case both copies are from only one parent.

DNA The physical substance of genetic material. Mostly junk.

Double helix The structure of DNA, consisting of two helices wound around each other. More than twice the fun of a single helix.

Gametes Sex cells such as eggs, sperm, or pollen (in plants). Useful term for ordering breakfast, as in "Gametes and bacon, please."

Gene Unit of inheritance consisting of a segment of DNA. Something that can be convenient to blame for your idiosyncrasies. The sequence of codons that specifies a protein.

Genes Plural of gene. Not to be confused with Levis.

Gene chip Research tool to detect when genes are turned on or off. Taste better with salt and vinegar (U.K.), or cheese and salsa (U.S.).

Genetic code a) how sets of three DNA bases correspond to building blocks of gene products (i.e. amino acids); b) the secret language of geneticists.

Genome The full set of genes and DNA in an organism. Sounds like, but is not to be confused with, statues of bearded men found in gardens.

Heredity Transmission of biological characteristics from parent to child. Explains why you are more like your parents than you care to admit.

Heritability The geneticists' attempt to quantify how much of something can be blamed on genes vs. being dropped on your head as a child.

Junk DNA DNA for which the function is Not Yet Known. Present in great abundance in politicians, co-workers and relatives you dislike.

Locus The location of a particular gene on a chromosome. In the world of hereditary real estate, it's locus, locus, locus.

Megabase One million bases. Not to be confused with enormous speakers for your sound system.

Molecules The smallest unit of a chemical that can still maintain its unique qualities. Examples include fats, sugars, DNA and proteins, in other words, what everyone happily eats for lunch.

Nucleotides Basic building blocks of DNA. Also used to refer to ocean currents caused by military submarines.

Phenotype What a living thing looks like, as in "Darling, I wasn't staring at the phenotype of that 18-year-old."

Recombination Exchange of DNA between pairs of chromosomes that produces new combinations of gene variants. Similar to what people do after they split up from a serious relationship.

Selfing The ability of certain plants to mate with themselves as they have both male and female sexual organs. Never admit to thinking about how this might work in anything but plants.

Sequencing Determining the order of bases – As, Ts, Cs, Gs – in DNA. Not to be confused with the approach some popular people have to dating.

SNP Single points in DNA that differ between individuals. When located in genes responsible for brain function can be the cause of opposing political views.

Wild type The most common version of a gene found in nature or in the standard laboratory stock of that species. What geneticists call each other if they do a risky experiment.

THE AUTHOR

Gwen Acton was nurtured in Philadelphia where she variously tried to determine if her nature was to be a glamorous movie star, a professional athlete, or a multi-billionaire. Instead, she studied biology at the University of Pennsylvania, where the high point of her undergraduate career was observing small monkeys communicate with each other by rubbing smelly bodily fluids on various objects in their environment.

As a graduate student, she spent six long years counting the mutant offspring of microscopically small round worms. For introducing them to a new gene (that turned parts of them blue), the Massachusetts Institute of Technology (M.I.T.) awarded her a doctorate in biology. In a superb bluff she was then hired by Harvard University to inflict genetics and introductory biology on its undergraduate population – for which the inheritance implications have yet to be fully determined.

She runs a business consulting practice near Boston and in her spare time she tries to grow green and yellow peas in her garden which (fittingly) primarily support the local rabbit population in its breeding efforts.

The Cosmos

To start any conversation with "In the known universe" is a good ploy that makes you sound smart because it hints at your awareness of an even vaster 'unknown' one. Similarly, saying "Our universe" acknowledges there could be others next door, as it were.

Men:

Men run faster because they have a narrower pelvis, which means that when running they need to rotate it less fast than women in proportion to the distance covered. It also means that no man can walk like Marilyn Monroe.

Music:

The only fruitful line of discussion on Beethoven is with regard to the comparative merits of the symphonies. The concertos are rarely mentioned, especially the Emperor and the Violin Concerto because they are both perfect and popular and lead the conversation nowhere.

Life Coaching:

The life coachee will need to be helped to separate and address the urgent before the merely important, and warned not to spend so much time separating these two categories of activities that suddenly everything becomes urgent.

Sex:

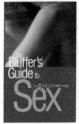

A cursory look at the design and anatomical positioning of the male and female sexual organs shows that when God designed *Homo sapiens*, aestheticism and ease of access were not high on the job description.

Negotiation:

In order to secure a bargain in which you get what is important and concede what is trivial, it helps immeasurably if you can distinguish one from the other. The best negotiators will create a lengthy squabble about a trivial point, with every intention of conceding it.

On the series:

"The biggest bluff about The Bluffer's Guides series is the title. In fact, these books contain, in capsulated form, an astonishing amount of information anyone may profit from." *The Daily Telegraph*

Philosophy:

"A great little book with just enough information to be intriguing. It's funny even if you know nothing about philosophy but, the more familiar you are with the players, the more amusing it is." Reader from Kew Gardens, N.Y., U.S.

Psychology:

"I loved this book from start to finish. It had me chortling and has whetted my appetite to learn more." Reader from Seattle

Marketing:

"The best marketing book ever. I still regularly read my copy (just to check!) and give copies to new starts in marketing (and old hands who should know better). One read through will tell you more than any course by a 'marketing guru'." Reader from London

the Bluffer's® Guides

Oval Books

*This Bluffer's® Guide is available as a downloadable
audiobook: **www.audible.co.uk/bluffers**

We like to hear from our readers.
Please send us your views on our books
and we will publish them as appropriate on
our web site: ovalbooks.com.

Oval Books also publish the best-selling
Xenophobe's Guide® series –
see www.ovalbooks.com

Both series can be bought via Amazon or directly
from us, Oval Books through our web site
www.ovalbooks.com or by contacting us.

Oval Books charges the full cover price
for its books (because they're worth it) and
£2.00 for postage and packing on the first
book. Buy a second book or more and postage
and packing will be entirely FREE.

To order by post please fill out the accompanying
order form and send to:
Oval Books
5 St John's Buildings
Canterbury Crescent
London SW9 7QH

cheques should be made payable to: Oval Books

or phone us on +44 (0)20 7733 8585
or visit our web site at: www.ovalbooks.com

Payment may be made by Visa or Mastercard and orders are
dispatched as soon as the card details and mailing address are
received. If the mailing address is not the same as the card holder's
address it is necessary to give both.

Oval Books